Animals in Danger

David Black

Macdonald Educational

Contents

How to use this book

This book tells you about animals that are in danger of dying out forever. It tells you what happened to them in the past and what might happen to them in the future. You will discover some of the places they live in and some of the problems they face. Look first at the contents page to see if the subject you are interested in is listed. For example, if you are interested in elephants, you will find them on pages 18 and 19. The index will tell you where and how many times a particular subject is mentioned and if there is a picture of it. A white pelican, for example, is to be found on pages 24 and 25.

Page

6 **Man the vandal**
Natural extinction of animals. Man's rise to power and his increase in population.

8 **Animal homes**
Where different animals live and why they live there. Delicate natural balances.

10 **Save the forests!**
How we are cutting down the forests of the world. The debt we must pay.

12 **Rare jungle animals**
Some of the animals that may vanish if we do not look after them and their forests.

14 **American grasslands**
How the bison nearly disappeared. What happened in the South American pampas.

16 **The African savannah**
Animals in competition with man. Animals hunted for sport.

18 **African elephants and poachers**
The trade in ivory and a disappearing giant.

20 **Desert animals in danger**
Hunting with machine guns, jeeps and airplanes. The numbat and blackbuck.

22 **Wetlands**
Unpleasant for people, a natural haven for wildlife.

24 **Birds of the wetlands**
Pelicans and cranes.

26 **Island life in the oceans**
The most threatened wildlife. Galapagos, Madagascar and the Mascarenes.

28 **The seas must live!**
How the seas are being polluted. Oil tanker disasters. Dolphins we accidently kill.

30 **Save the whale!**
Commercial hunting on a huge scale. The many uses we have for whales.

32 **Sea animals**
The harp seal; slaughter on the ice. Turtles for food, turtles for souvenirs.

34 **The case of the vanishing toad**
A case history of the natterjack toad in England and its rescue.

36 **The tiger**
Man-eaters. Trophy hunters. The Lord of the Jungle in danger. 'Operation Tiger', a case study.

38 **Trade in death**
Animals hunted for their skins and meat. Animals exported for pet shops. Animals that die in shipment. Substitutes for wild animal products.

40 **Breeding and reintroduction**
How zoos can help. How we can return animals to their homelands.

42 **What you can do to help**
Local conservation. Looking after our countryside. How you can attract wild animals into your garden.

44 **Books to read, things to do, places to go**

45 **A danger list**
839 endangered animals.

46 **Index**

Man the vandal

Life on earth has been continually changing ever since it began at least two billion years ago. Some kinds of animals die out, new species appear. It is a natural process. Fossils found in different rock levels tell us when certain animals flourished. For example, dinosaurs were the dominant animals for 155 million years. That age ended 70 million years ago and the Age of Mammals, which we live in now, began. Although man has lived on earth for a few million years, it is only in the last few hundred years that he has really begun to change and damage his surroundings.

Man becomes powerful

Man progressed from food gatherer and hunter until about 10,000 years ago when he began to farm animals and crops. For the first time man had a real sense of home. By the 1300s man's power and numbers had greatly increased. He began to cut down the forests for fuel, land and timber to build houses and boats. Soon he wanted to explore new lands and continents.

The past two hundred years have seen small towns grow into huge cities. With the use of steam power, machines and electricity, man has begun to control and shape his environment.

The last wild quagga was shot in 1878. South African farmers thought quaggas were pests that competed with their cattle for grass.

White men with rifles nearly hunted the bison to extinction to feed armies of railroad builders. Later shot for sport, the bodies were often left to rot.

The villian of this book is man. But animals also die out from natural causes, like these mammoths stuck in a tar pit. Other causes of extinction could be a change in climate or unsuccessful competition with other animals. Natural extinction leaves room for new species to thrive; animals killed-off by man will never be replaced.

Are we too late?

Man's rise in importance has been sudden and dramatic. In the search for food, raw materials and space to house his ever increasing numbers man has slaughtered animals, steamrollered the land and vandalised the forests and natural vegetation. Massacres of seals or elephants remind us of our savage cruelty to animals. More dangerous however for the animals is the way the natural world is being destroyed. The vanished forests, the drained wetlands and the polluted seas were all the homes of animals.

A few primitive peoples live in harmony with nature. The rest of us do not. Our greed and stupidity seem endless. Can we learn before it is too late?

The growth of towns in the Industrial Revolution ate up land and polluted the country. ▼

Animal homes

Ecology is the study of environments. Environments are, quite simply, all the things that surround us. The main ingredients of an environment are climate (wind, rain and sun), soil, plants and the animals living there. A town environment will be made up of concrete, buildings, smoke, cars and people. Animals live in environments too, but most of them live outside of the towns. An environment includes lots of habitats. These are the particular places each animal lives in. For example, the frog's habitat is the pond, whilst the mole's is under the ground and the fieldmouse lives in fields and hedges.

Ecosystems

Ecosystems describe all the living parts and non-living parts (soil and climate) of a habitat. All these parts work together and depend on each other. It is a bit like a giant jigsaw puzzle. Plants and animals have slowly adapted themselves to fit into this pattern of life. If any one part

Energy cycle of the African savannah. All life depends on energy from the sun which is changed into simple food substances. Plant-eating animals like the termite and hartebeests are in turn eaten by meat-eaters. The remains of animals and dung break down into the soil and the goodness is reused to help plants grow.

meat-eaters (lion)

scavengers (vulture)

plant-eaters (hartebeeste)

insect-eaters (ant-eater)

insects (termites)

of the ecosystem suddenly changes, all the other parts will be affected, sometimes drastically.

An ecosystem can be as small as a rotten tree trunk or as big as a park. Natural balances developed between plants and animals are very delicate. They are easily unbalanced. In this book we shall see the effects on wildlife that result from man changing or destroying parts of ecosystems.

Natural vegetation zones

The earth is divided into areas of natural vegetation. Ecologists call them *biomes*. Their form depends on the shape of the land, its height above sea-level, soil, climate and distance from the equator.

Over thousands of years animals have gradually become adapted to these different worlds. Forest animals live in and around trees whilst desert animals avoid the heat and save water. Marine animals, especially fish, have become adapted to eat, breathe and reproduce under water. Animals even became adapted to live in the permanent coldness of the polar regions.

World vegetation map. These *biomes* do not have fixed boundaries, they overlap and change with time. These areas are very fragile and easily damaged. Nowhere is untouched by man, he has affected all of them. Some animals have become adapted to these changes, others, that have not, are some of the 'animals in danger'.

- Permanent ice and tundra
- Coniferous forest
- Temperate forest
- Grassland
- Tropical forest
- Desert and scrub

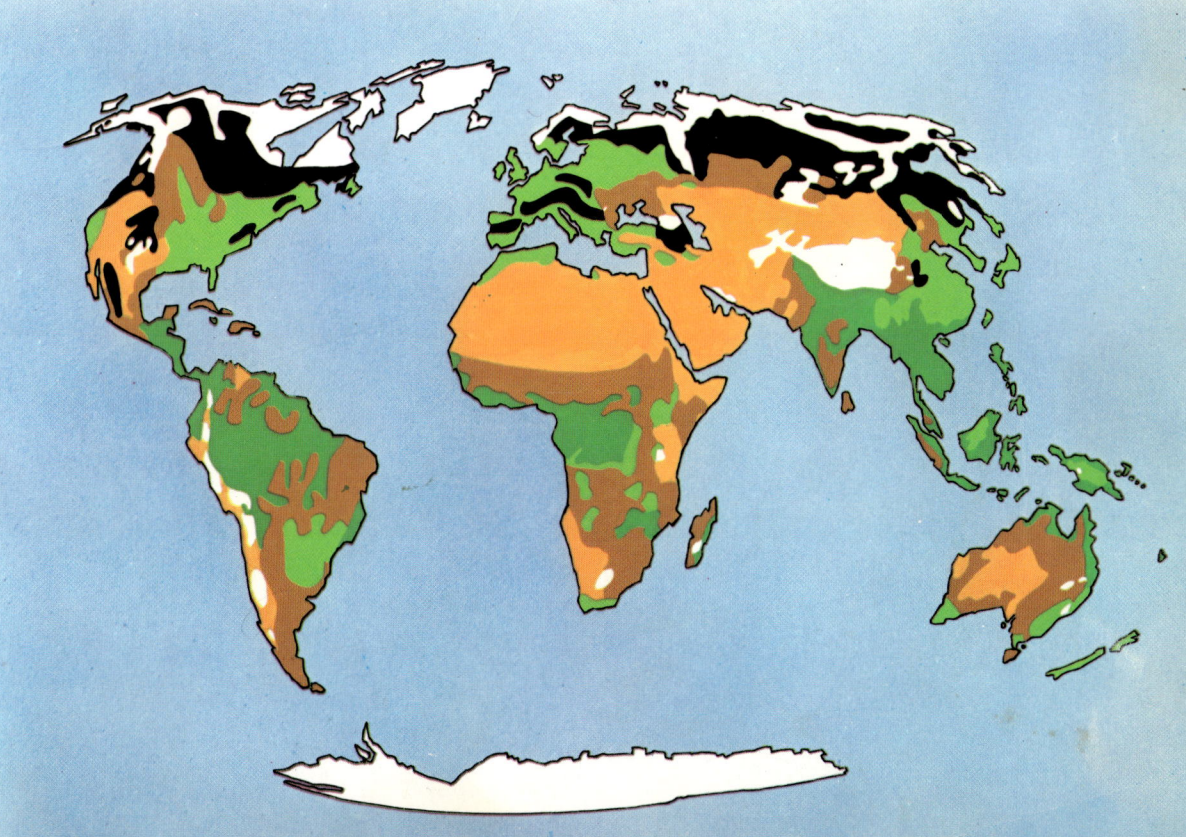

Tropical forests are natural timber sources. Hardwood, mahogany and teak, is exported all over the world. More trees are cleared for rubber or coffee plantations, while mining works have scarred huge areas of forest.

Save the forests!

Twenty-five years ago satellite pictures would have shown tropical rain forests as non-stop green belts across South America, Africa and Southeast Asia. Today, similar pictures show huge patches where trees have been hacked away and cleared. This destruction goes on at an alarming rate of 20 hectares every minute, every day of the year. For example, forest land about the size of England was lost building the Trans-Amazonica highway in Brazil.

A rich world of animals

The tropical forest is the richest natural area of plants and animals. This hot and steamy world with no real seasons is full of life; giant butterflies; bright orchids sprouting from trees; colourful birds screeching in the trees. Trees are cut down for timber, forests are cleared for farms or mines. These are the downfall of the forest.

Exploiting the forest

Most jungle trees have tall slim trunks with foliage at the top like giant umbrellas. Few plants grow on the gloomy ground. The soil is not very fertile, it needs the richness from rotted leaves falling from the trees. When trees are felled, there are no more leaves to fall. The soil loses the shade of the trees, dries out and loses its goodness. Without trees to shield it from the tropical rain storms, the weak soil washes away easily. As much as 34 tonnes per hectare is lost each year this way.

Land cleared for farming is not productive for long. Farmers soon have to move on and clear *more* trees to grow enough crops. So the destruction goes on. Rubber, bananas, cocoa and chemicals from plants are just a few of the many things we get from the forest. These forests, which have existed for many millions of years, have much to offer us. If we do not stop and think *now* they will be gone by the end of the century. Not only will the animals disappear, but also the primitive peoples who also live in the jungle. They are also dying-out as their homes and ways of life are destroyed.

The world's last great jungle wilderness was opened up by the 5,000 km long Trans-Amazonica highway. Along it have grown settlements with all the ill effects of civilization. The 'green hell' of early explorers has been tamed.

◀ One reason the orang-utan is in danger is because it is so rare! The rarer it becomes, the more people want it as a pet. It lives in the forests of Borneo and Sumatra.

▲ The South American quetzal was often hunted for its feathers. The main threat to it is the loss of its forest habitat where the quetzal finds a constant supply of the small fruits it eats.

Queen Alexandra's birdwing is the largest butterfly in the world. Its wingspan can be over 20 centimetres. Collectors, who will pay hundreds of pounds for a single specimen, endanger it. ▶

Rare jungle animals

You might be disappointed exploring a tropical forest in daytime. You might expect snakes to be curled on every branch and the air filled with blood-curdling noises, but it can be strangely deserted. This is because many forest animals are active only at night and many live high up in trees, often out of sight in the canopy of leaves. Here tiny tree frogs breed in rainwater that collects in plants growing on the giant trees. Monkeys high up eat fruit and leaves in company with brightly coloured birds. The endless variety of animals crowding the jungles make these forests the richest habitats on earth. There are so many South American jungle animals that scientists have not yet even named them all!

Jungle animals across the world

A whole world of animals and plants dies when a forest is destroyed. Most animals are restricted to certain parts of the forest and are not very widespread. Each continent has its own unique forest creatures including many endangered ones. For example, South America has macaws, marmosets, jaguars and ocelots. Africa has gorillas, the Congo peacock and strange rock fowl. In South East Asia there are gibbons and the Sumatran rhinoceros, whilst New Guinea has the exotic crowned pigeon.

Nature reserves

Many countries have established nature reserves and wildlife parks. Some have been more successful than others. The main problem is people wanting land for other uses, apart from protecting animals.

▲ The Southeast Asian pileated gibbon's forest habitat is being destroyed. This agile ape can leap as far as 12 metres. It is protected in one small park in Thailand.

▲ The magnificent monkey-eating eagle lives only in the Philippines. It is rare because it is shot and stuffed as a trophy.

The very rare woolly spider monkey lives in the dense forests of Brazil. Few zoos have managed to keep them alive. None has ever been able to breed them. ▶

The golden tree frog is found only in an 800 hectare area of Panama. Tourists buy these bright yellow frogs as living souvenirs. Although it is illegal, the frogs are also exported. ▼

American grasslands

Imagine the great prairies of North America 400 years ago—vast tracts of sweeping grassland, almost deserted. A distant rumbling sound gets gradually louder, then on the horizon one sees a mass of moving black bodies—bison!

What happened to the bison?

In 1700 about 60 million roamed the prairies in relative peace. They had few natural enemies; only man and grizzly bears hunted them. The Cheyenne and Cree were two Indian tribes that depended on bison for their livelihood. They used every bit of the bison, even the hooves and sinews. They hunted only when meat was needed and were not a real threat to the huge herds. It was European settlers, 'Wild West' pioneers, who almost wiped out the bison. 1873 saw 4 million killed; in under a year and a half 'Buffalo Bill' killed 4,000. By 1890 less than 9,000 were left. The settlers' cattle had taken over the plains the bison once inhabited. Today you can see protected bison in some National Parks.

Smaller prairie animals

Bison eat plants. As the bison died out, more grass was available for smaller plant eaters and their populations rose. But not for long—farmers shot or poisoned them as they competed for grass with their cattle. A major victim was the black-tailed prairie dog.

As the black-footed ferret preys on prairie dogs and lives in their burrows, it in turn was endangered and is now possibly the rarest American mammal.

▲ The elegant maned wolf is very shy, it feeds on small animals and also fruit.

Prairie dogs and their 'towns' use up valuable cattle grazing land. ▼

Animals of the pampas

The pampas is a huge grassland area of South America; it occupies about 80 million hectares of Argentina. Until the last century few people lived there, only nomadic Indians. Today it is an important sheep and cattle farming area. Like the prairie today, no large wild animals live there.

The rhea is a flightless bird once hunted by the gauchos with a 'bolas' which is a kind of lasso weighted with stones. Rheas have become rarer but some survive on large farms. Rare mammals include the pampas deer, a small elegant animal, less than 300 survive. The maned wolf is very rare and very shy. It was easily frightened by the farmers and was forced to retreat to the northern edges of the pampas. It is now protected to stop its numbers falling any more.

A gaucho driving cattle across the vast pampas plain. Large scale cattle farming caused a fall in numbers of many animals. The pampas deer may be so rare because many died from diseases, like foot and mouth disease that they caught from domestic animals. A small herd of pampas deer is protected on a private ranch.

giant sable antelope

leopard

The African savannah

A great variety of animals lives in the huge African National Parks. The savannah grasslands and deserts that border them are especially rich in wildlife. However, many familiar animals are dying out. One, which lives on the edges of the savannah, is Grevy's zebra. Large herds once roamed the dry Northern Kenya grasslands. They became rare when they were hunted for their skins. Good skins fetch up to £600 in luxury shops abroad. Although local poachers get nothing like this for the skins, they still make a lot of money hunting zebra.

The savannah scene here shows the animals mentioned in the text. They would not normally be found living in exactly the same area.

African wild ass

white rhinoceros

The white rhinoceros

The northern group of white rhinoceros may be almost extinct, but thanks to protective measures, the southern group is safe. Rhinos are shot for their horns which are sold to some people in the Far East who believe they can cure all sorts of diseases.

The cheetah is also on the danger list; fewer than 20,000 remain in Africa. This animal needs plenty of space to hunt and breed in. Man and his cattle easily disturb the cheetah and cause it to move to new hunting grounds. Another big cat, the leopard, is more widespread, but also falling in numbers. It is shot because it kills domestic animals and also for its beautiful fur which is made into very expensive fashion coats.

A giant antelope

Less familiar animals in danger include the Angolan giant sable antelope. Shot as big game, its superb horns are over 1.5 m long. Its population may be as low as 30,000.

In 1905 there were over 10,000 African wild asses. Today there are a few hundred. They live in the Somali semi-desert where little grass grows. Domestic animals compete for this grass and make it hard for the ass to survive. Tribesmen hunt the ass as they think its fat can cure tuberculosis!

African elephants and poachers

The elephant is the largest living land mammal, it is also very intelligent. It has a strong family life and lives up to 70 years. Sadly, it now faces a crisis. Recent surveys show a minimum of 1,250,000 living in the African continent. This seems a lot, but fifty years ago there were very many more. Then the elephant was common in almost all African countries south of the equator.

Elephants are very adaptable. They live in a wide variety of habitats—forests, grasslands, river valleys and desert scrub. They eat many different foods such as grass, twigs, leaves, roots and fruit.

Three threats to the elephant

Three things threaten the elephant. Firstly, its natural habitat is being used up for farming and forestry. The second threat is damage caused to vegetation when too many elephants live in one area. Such large animals need lots of food and in some National Parks dense elephant populations have killed off the trees by stripping and eating their bark. The third and most serious threat, though, is elephant hunting for meat in West Africa, and for ivory in East and Central Africa. The price of ivory has gone up so much that hunting elephants for their tusks has become 'big business'. For example, at least 100,000 were killed in 1976 for their ivory. There are now international laws to control the import and export of ivory goods, but they are only a start in the battle to stop the elephant slaughter. Smugglers often avoid these laws. Sometimes even African government officials make money from the ivory trade.

Elephant populations

Elephant numbers continue to fall in some countries like Kenya and Uganda, while countries like Tanzania have steady populations. One problem throughout Africa is that herds may become isolated from each other. If these separate herds become too small, there will be little chance of interbreeding. This in turn makes it even more difficult for the elephants to survive.

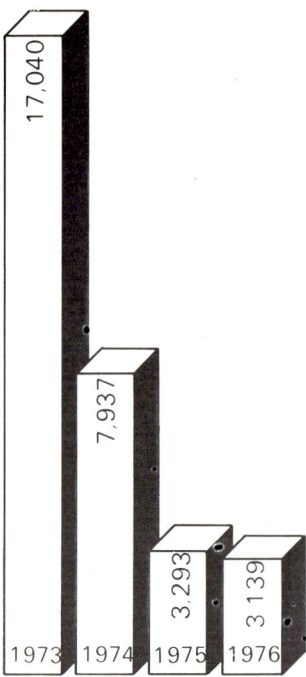

▲ Even in National Parks elephants are not safe. This graph shows the fall in their numbers in two Ugandan parks.

IVORY FACTS AND FIGURES

The price of ivory in the 1960s was up to $22 (US) a kilo. By the mid 70s it was $110 (US).

In 1977 international trade in carved and finished ivory was worth about $38,000,000 (US). Hong Kong was responsible for 80% of this figure.

Kenya exported under 20 tonnes of ivory in the 1920s. By 1977 the figure was estimated at 250 tonnes.

From 1970–77 elephant numbers in Kenya fell by 50%.

Ivory exports from all of Africa in 1977 meant the death of 60,000 elephants.

Poisoned arrows kill elephants in 12 hours. Poachers track them until the beasts collapse and die.

Wardens use radios and jeeps to track poachers. Often a few men must patrol thousands of square kilometres.

Trophies and carved ivory are popular with tourists in Africa; even the feet are used as waste-paper baskets.

Desert animals in danger

You might think animals would be safe in the desert wastes. Many, like snakes and insects, *are* safe, but many of the larger animals, especially antelopes, are in danger. One of the most dramatic stories is that of the Arabian oryx, a handsome whiteish antelope with great long horns. This oryx has always been hunted by Arab people. It was a sign of courage and manhood to kill one. Arab men believed that eating the beast's flesh would make them so strong that even bullets could not harm them. Today this is just history, for the oryx is extinct as a wild animal in its homeland. Early this century people began to hunt them in motor vehicles. Instead of an exciting hunt riding on camels, men now chased oryx until the animals fell dead with exhaustion. In the 60s the Arabs even hunted them from airplanes. No wild oryx have been reported alive since 1974.

Operation Oryx

Luckily, there are more Arabian oryx living elsewhere. Over 200 are kept in North American zoos. Most were bred from wild animals captured in 1962 in an imaginative rescue plan called 'Operation Oryx'. Three wild oryx were flown out to Phoenix Zoo in Arizona, later others arrived. Now they form the basis of a healthy breeding herd. By 1978 some had even been taken back to Jordan where they were also once wild.

The scimitar-horned oryx and the addax

The rare scimitar-horned oryx has even longer horns than the Arabian oryx. It lives on the southern edge of the Sahara desert and is also threatened by hunters. It does not help that domestic cattle graze its pastures and leave it little to eat.

The strange looking addax has peculiar twisted horns. It lives on the remote Saharan sand dunes. It cannot run so fast as many antelopes. Soldiers armed with machine guns hunted them from jeeps. People working on local oil fields shot them for sport and amusement and continued the pointless slaughter.

Arabian oryx

addax

The horns of the Arabian oryx and addax are prized as trophies. The addax is a perfect desert animal, it never drinks as it gets all the water it needs from desert plants it eats.

▲ Dogs, rats and other animals introduced by early settlers caused the decline of some Australian marsupials. The numbat is one of the most attractive of these. It is active in daytime and feeds only on termites. Once common in South Australia it is only found today in parts of south-west Australia.

The blackbuck, one of the world's fastest animals, lives in the desert areas of India. In the last 50 years it has been hunted with modern firearms. The large spiral horns of the male blackbuck are considered a great trophy. Now, it is almost extinct in India and rare in neighbouring Pakistan. A captive herd of over 5,000 blackbuck has been built up on the dry prairie-lands of Texas in North America. ▶

Wetlands

Wetlands include marshes and bogs, swamps and estuaries. They may not be nice for us to walk in or live in, but they are very important places for wildlife. If you look at a map of Europe, it is hard to find wetlands marked, as they are often small. Despite their small size, many different plants and animals live there; birds, frogs, fishes, worms and insects, the list is almost endless. If you have a microscope at school, look at a drop of pondwater. You will see it is full of life.

The giant otter of South America is threatened because it is shot for its fur.

Draining the marshes

Unfortunately, wetlands are not very popular with people. In the tropics especially, wetlands are often breeding grounds for animals and insects, like mosquitoes, which carry diseases. Very often wetlands are drained for farming or building on. The need for land in Europe is so great that many of these areas are rapidly vanishing.

As they are such unpleasant places for people, wetlands are often quite wild and untouched. Because of this they are important in many ways. Many ducks, geese and wading birds use them as winter feeding grounds. These birds breed in the far north of Europe or Russia. In autumn they fly south in huge flocks to

Scarring the landscape—a coastal wetland with power station in background.

The black lechwe lives only in a 160 kilometre wide swamp in Zambia.

where the weather is warmer and where the wetlands are not frozen over. Here they can feed before returning north again in spring. For example, if the Wexford Slobs in Ireland were drained, half the world's population of white-fronted geese would be in danger. Estuaries are important shallow feeding waters for young fish. Some, like flounders, are eaten by man.

The wild Camargue

The Camargue is an area of salt marshes and lagoons in southern France. It is a strange wild place full of creatures like flamingoes and wild horses. Its wild beauty attracts over 1,500,000 visitors each year. If, for example, it was drained to grow rice, the wildlife would disappear and with it the money spent by tourists. Many local people's livelihoods would suffer as a result.

Pollution of the wetlands

Wetlands also suffer from chemical pollution. Chemical waste from factories and farm fertilizers drain into rivers and the rivers carry them down to the estuaries. This process badly affected wildlife in the Norfolk Broads. Fertilizers drained into the rivers and caused an unnatural growth of plants. This in turn clogged up the waterways and killed or suffocated fish and small water creatures.

A wetland paradise—the Everglades, a swampy part of southern Florida.

spoonbill

Manchurian crane

white pelican

All these beautiful and fascinating wetland birds are threatened by man.

Birds of the wetlands

The people who value wetlands most are bird lovers because throughout the year these marshy places are alive with many kinds of birds. Some birds come to breed in the spring or summer whilst some fly in to feed from colder parts during autumn and winter. Curlews, coots, moorhens, bitterns, swans, ducks, geese, little grebes, reeves and waders are just some of the birds that feed and nest among wetland plants.

Rare European birds

There are several kinds of rare wetland birds in Europe, including two types of pelican—the Dalmatian pelican and the white pelican—both found in south-east Europe and the Danube Delta in Rumania. The delta is a fascinating watery world of marshes, islands and marsh plants. It is home for two other exotic-looking birds, the glossy ibis and the white spoonbill, which are also rare in Europe.

The squacco heron, another inhabitant of the reed beds, is fortunately increasing in numbers. During the last century thousands of these elegant little birds were killed for their head feathers. These were used to decorate the hats of fashionable ladies of the time. This practice has now stopped and the squacco heron is protected by law. One other rare bird of the delta is the pygmy cormorant. This bird has a red-brown head and is much smaller than other cormorants.

The beautiful cranes

Even more spectacular than the delta birds are cranes. These handsome long-legged birds mostly live in wet places and many are extremely rare. For example there are less than seventy whooping cranes left in the world. As far as we know all of these nest in the marshy areas of Wood Buffalo National Park in north-west Canada. Every year this last flock of cranes migrates over 2,500 miles south to spend the winter on the coastal marshes of Texas. At the moment experiments are being carried out to try and rear young 'whoopers' in the nests of the more common sandhill crane.

The Manchurian crane

From the Far East comes another interesting story—that of the beautiful white and black Manchurian crane. The last known survivors of mainland Asia's Manchurian cranes have found shelter in the no-man's land between North and South Korea. In this peaceful setting once torn apart by bombs and bullets, the cranes find ideal feeding conditions. The Manchurian crane is a symbol of long-life and happiness to the people of the East. Local inhabitants now encourage them by leaving food —grain and rice—so that they can feed before moving on. There are probably less than 150 of these birds alive throughout their range from Korea, north through China and Manchuria to Arctic Russia.

Dalmatian pelicans and white pelicans are threatened by the destruction of the reed beds where they live and breed. They are also killed by fishermen. Pelicans fish together in groups of six or eight. They swim in formation and every few metres open all their mouths at the same time. Any fish nearby are caught. This means they eat a lot of fish which leaves less for the fishermen. One place where they can still be seen in numbers is the Danube Delta in Rumania. Here they are protected by the government. ▼

▲ Once eaten by sailors for their meat, the giant Galapagos tortoises are now protected by law.

▲ The marine iguana is another Galapagos animal. This reptile eats seaweed.

▲ The flightless takahe of New Zealand is now found in only one isolated valley.

Island life in the oceans

Islands are fascinating wildlife areas. Some islands have been cut off from the mainland for millions of years, others were never part of it. Many strange types of animals and plants, found nowhere else, live on these islands. The Galapagos Islands, 1,100 km off Ecuador, were visited by Charles Darwin in 1835. He saw many types of finches living there. Each type had a different beak. He thought that a single sort of finch had strayed from the mainland to the islands. The birds had no competition on the islands apart from themselves. Their numbers rose on the small islands. Food was limited, so they became adapted to new foods. Some eventually ate only insects, others only berries or seeds or fruits. Each beak was suited to eating only one type of food. Darwin's study of the finches and other animals, like iguanas, led to his theory of evolution.

Why island animals are in the greatest danger

Island animals are more threatened than other animals. The largest number of extinct animals came from islands. The main threat has been the arrival of man and the animals that came with him; dogs, cats, rats, goats and pigs. Often few large meat-eaters lived on islands. Local animals were easy prey for the new animals. Goats and cattle helped destroy the vegetation. Man completed the process by clearing the land for farms and homes. This happened in the Mascarene Islands in the Indian Ocean. Ship rats came with the first sailors. The rats easily grew in numbers and soon threatened local birdlife. Today, out of 45 different kinds of birds once living on these islands, only 21 remain now.

No retreat for the island animals

Island animals have nowhere to go if their habitats are threatened. Islands are often very small. Another problem is that island animals may be adapted to eat food found only on their island. They become as highly specialized as Darwin's finches. If the food they eat is destroyed, so are the animals.

Madagascar island (Malagasy Republic) has been cut off from Africa for millions of years. Its unique vegetation supports equally unique animals, many which could not live anywhere else. Most of these strange animals live in forests. As 80% of the forest has been cleared, especially for banana plantations, all these animals are in danger. The island is well-known for primitive primates called lemurs.

Verreaux's sifaka is one of the last 20 types of lemur in Madagascar. It is most active in daytime. This spectacular animal leaps over 10 metres among the trees of the western forests. ▼

▲ The woolly avahi is an animal that is active at night and rarely leaves the trees. It eats leaves, fruit and bark. Its young cling to its breast.

The false sunbird may already be extinct. It hovers by flowers and eats the nectar and insects there.

The elephant bird was over 2.2 metres high, its egg was bigger than a football! It died out in 1649. ▶

The seas must live

Almost three-quarters of the world's surface is covered by oceans. The sea affects our climate and the life of plants and animals on land. It also gives us high protein food in the form of fish and shellfish. But the seas are being polluted and abused. As we do not live there, we can easily forget the harm we are doing. It is easy to think that oceans are endless and bottomless. They are not. By the year 2000 an estimated 6,000 million people will live on earth. We shall need the oceans more and more as a source of food and energy if *we* are to survive.

The world's dustbin

We tip ever increasing amounts of waste into the seas. They have become huge rubbish dumps. A lot of this waste is hard to break down naturally. It chokes and poisons much marine life. However, much of this is hidden from us, we only see a small part of the damage. For example, beautiful coral reefs in Hawaii have been killed by sewage pollution. Other reefs suffer in different ways—they may be choked by dumped waste or dredged mud.

Rubbish on European beaches stretches from the North Sea to the Mediterranean. This is ugly and it is also very dangerous. Fish are found choked to death on plastic cups thrown from cross-Channel ferries.

Oil pollution

The danger to wildlife from oil slicks is often in the news. Seabirds are the most obvious casualties—especially diving

Anti rubbish-dumping laws are easy to avoid if no one is watching. It is hard to control ships far out at sea.

birds like auks and guillemots. Their feathers become coated with oil. This lets water soak into the feathers and they become waterlogged so the birds cannot fly. One bird, the long-tailed duck, seems to deliberately settle on oil slicks. Perhaps it mistakes the oil for a shoal of fish—a disastrous mistake!

Overfishing

Overfishing is another danger. Most people from Western Europe and North America tend to eat just a few types of fish, like cod and haddock. These few types are heavily fished until very few remain. The UK was involved in a 'war' with Iceland over the rights to fish cod in the North Sea. In fact, there are many other edible fish in the area that are hardly fished at all.

Eventually, the fish we prefer to eat begin to disappear and we are forced to turn to new types of fish. One of these,

▲ These men are cleaning up oil spilt on French beaches when the tanker Amoco Cadiz broke up on nearby rocks in 1978.

Oil pollution killed this young gannet. Even the chemicals used to clean up oil spills may endanger wildlife. ▼

the capelin, lives in the cold Arctic waters. Although capelin fishing is a recent development, already 500,000 tonnes are caught each year. This massive harvest cannot go on forever. The capelin is also the staple diet of fin whales and harp seals. Once it is gone, the animals feeding on it must find new food sources. Probably these will not be enough and the animals will simply starve.

Animals we kill by accident

Marine animals may also be indirect victims of fishing activities. Each year about 90,000 spotted dolphins, 50,000 spinner dolphins and 20,000 Dall's porpoises are killed accidently. Tuna fishermen deliberately look for these animals because they know they will find tuna fish near them. Dolphins and porpoises get caught in the tuna nets and are later thrown away. This is particularly common in the Pacific where tuna are fished.

Save the whale!

Whales are astonishing animals. The blue whale is the largest of them all. It grows up to 30 metres long and can weigh 150 tonnes. Whales are a group of sea mammals whose ancestors left the land over 60 million years ago. There are over 30 different kinds of large whales as well as many smaller dolphins and porpoises. They are very intelligent animals and communicate with each other by a large range of sounds. The beautiful and haunting 'song' of the hump-back whale can last up to 30 minutes without repeating sounds. They are then accurately repeated. The white whale has even been called the 'sea canary'.

Whale hunting

The Basque peoples of northern Spain were the first to hunt whales on a big scale. They hunted the 'right' whale, so-called because it was the right whale to catch as it swam close to the shore. Since then whaling has become a highly efficient industry. Whales are detected by radar, killed by explosive harpoons and cut up at sea on special factory ships.

Whales have many uses. The great baleen whales are hunted for their oil, meat, blood and bones. Whale oil, especially the sperm whale's, is of the highest quality. It is used as a lubricant in industry and motor cars. It is also used to soften some leather. The Japanese consider whale meat a delicacy. The poorer meat cuts are used to make pet food. (Whale margarine and petfoods are banned in the UK). Sperm whales are also hunted for the spermaceti wax found in their heads. This is widely used in cosmetics. High quality soaps and perfumes often contain ambergris, a substance found in the intestines of the sperm whale.

Whaling laws

For the last 30 years the International Whaling Commission has tried to control whale hunting across the world. Some good has been done, but many people believe that the laws are not strong enough. They think hunting should completely stop for some years to let whales breed and build up their numbers.

We slaughter both whales and farm animals. Farm animals killed are replaced. We cannot replace whales. ▼

The harpoon tip explodes under the skin of the whale. The barbs expand and dig into the whale to keep hold of it. ▼

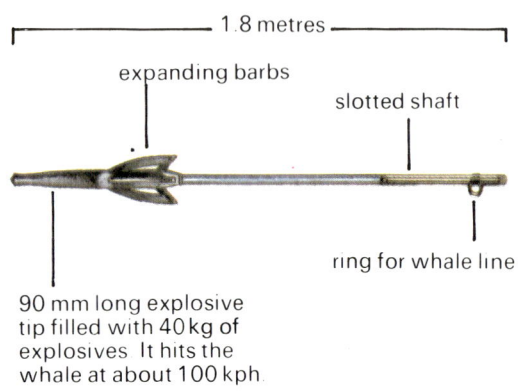

90 mm long explosive tip filled with 40 kg of explosives. It hits the whale at about 100 kph.

Estimated whale populations.
Original populations are *pre* commercial hunting. Commercial hunting greatly increased with the use of steam whalers (1864) and factory ships (1925).

Type of whale	Original population	Population today
Humpback	103,000	6,500
Sperm	975,000	560,000
Sei	180,000	86,000
Fin	475,000	90,000
Blue	205,000	6,000

Dall's porpoise; there are no reliable figures, but see page 29 for accidental deaths.

Dall's porpoise
maximum size 2.4 m

humpback whale
maximum size 15.2 m

sperm whale
maximum size 18.3 m

sei whale
maximum size 18.3 m

fin whale
maximum size 24.4 m

blue whale
maximum size 30 m

Only young harp seals have this lovely white fur. It is used for toys and furry knick-knacks.

Canadian harp seal population figures:
1949: 10,000,000
1979: 1,300,000
2009: ? ? ? ? ?

Sea animals

Seals are often in the news, especially young pups with large appealing eyes and cuddly coats; no wonder people get angry when they see them killed in films. The harp seal in Canada has had particular attention. Each year thousands of pups are slaughtered. People get very upset at the sight of the blood of dead seals. But what is the real situation? The simple answer is we don't know if the harp seal is in danger now, or in the future. The Canadian government allows this killing because it says the numbers of capelin fish have fallen greatly through seals eating them. It may be that the seals are not really responsible; maybe the real culprits are the fishermen whose livelihoods depend on fishing the capelin.

The Canadian government and the seal

Many people say that the Canadian government's decision to increase the number of seals killed each year to 180,000 will endanger the animal. It is also true that there are many seal hunters who depend on this annual kill for a living. One can argue that they could be employed elsewhere, but it is hard for people to change their jobs and life styles just because animal lovers tell them they ought to. It is easy to watch the television or read in the paper about the killing of rare animals, but what would *you* do if you lived there, how would *you* behave?

From the other side of the American continent comes a more optimistic story —that of the northern elephant seal, a monster up to 5 metres long and 3 tonnes in weight. In 1892 only about 100 of these seals were left alive. The rest had been killed for oil, boiled-out from their thick blubber. Today, thanks to protection, there are over 30,000. These seals spend most of the year at sea, coming in to land for only one month to breed and moult. One island they live on is the Ano Nuevo reserve just fifty miles south of San Francisco.

Turtles in danger

One cannot talk of rare sea creatures without mentioning turtles. Perhaps you have seen these strange reptiles in aquariums. The largest, and probably rarest, is the giant leathery turtle. The threat here is the collection of its eggs which are a rare delicacy in the Far East. The turtle drags itself up onto a beach where it scoops out a deep hole in the sand. It lays about 100 eggs. Often these are stolen as they are laid. The green turtle is killed both for its meat and shell. In Mexico, young turtles are killed, preserved and sold to tourists as souvenirs!

▲ The charming Californian sea otter is unpopular with fishermen because it feeds on the abalone, a large and tasty and valuable shellfish. It was hunted for its skin and was thought extinct by 1911. Luckily this was not so, since its rediscovery in 1938 it has been protected.

Young marine turtles are often killed and sold as souvenirs. Adults are killed for their meat, oil and shells. Their meat makes an expensive soup. ▼

toadspawn

tadpole

metamorphosis stage

The case of the vanishing toad

This is the story of the natterjack toad. Unlike the common toad found in gardens, the natterjack has a yellow stripe down its back. It lives in sandy places where it can burrow and near ponds where it can lay its eggs. Unfortunately, this bright little toad is so rare in Britain that it is now protected by law.

Ten years ago it was quite common on sandy heathland in southern England and along certain stretches of coastal sand dunes. Today its homes are much fewer. The decline of the toad is mainly due to disturbance by people. Roads and houses have been built over many of the heathlands, whilst many coastal areas it lives in are places where people go for weekends or picnics. Some heaths have been used for farm land. Others have been planted with valuable pine or spruce trees for timber. Unfortunately no money is made saving rare toads.

Holidaymakers versus the toad

Heaths are also the homes of two other interesting

Collecting toadspawn and tadpoles can endanger an already rare toad. ▼

animals—the sand lizard and the smooth snake. It is important that we should try and preserve these interesting parts of the countryside. Many organizations *are* trying to do this but it can be very difficult and complicated. Different people own different parts of the heaths. Each owner may use the land for different things—farms, factories, homes and so on. To preserve the habitat, all these people must be persuaded to help. The natterjack's coastal homes are also very popular with holiday makers—a holiday camp in the north-west has threatened one of the natterjack's last strongholds.

Helping the natterjack

Luckily organizations like the World Wildlife Fund and the Nature Conservancy Council are concerned about the natterjack. In Southport, Lancashire, mechanical diggers have been used to deepen the toad's breeding ponds behind the sand dunes. This gives the tadpoles a better chance of turning into young toads.

The dotted areas on the map show where the toad had retreated to by 1970. Before then it also lived in the black areas.

Save the natterjack! Deepening their ponds in north west England.

35

The tiger

British soldiers hunting tigers in India in the 19th century.

The tiger may be Lord of the Jungle, but it is equally at home near swamps or the cold Siberian forests. There are eight different types of tigers ranging from the small short-furred types to the larger and more powerful Siberian tiger. Large male Siberian tigers can weigh over 320 kg and be up to 4 metres long.

Man-eaters and trophies

All the different types of this truly magnificent animal are now rare wherever they live. One tiger which was found only on the island of Bali is extinct. In Southeast Asia vast areas of forest, the tiger's habitat, have been cleared for farms and to house the ever increasing human populations. Tigers have always been hunted for their lovely coats, their heads are stuffed for trophies. In the 1800s thousands of tigers were shot by Europeans in the colonies. Local people have always been afraid of 'man-eaters' which also attack domestic animals.

Operation Tiger

In 1972 the World Wildlife Fund started 'Operation Tiger', a campaign aimed at saving the tiger from extinction. This involved not only finding tigers and keeping them in reserves, but also trying to explain the plan to local people. Over £1,000,000 was raised and it helped pay for equipment, research scientists and forest guards.

Much of the operation was centred in India. Here nine reserves and three in nearby Nepal were set up specially to protect the tiger. Projects like this take a long time to work. At least there is now hope for tigers in India, where 50 years ago there were 40,000 and today perhaps only 2,500.

Europe has no wild tigers, but there is a slight chance that, not too far away, in south-east Turkey and northern Iraq a few may still be wild.

Today people are encouraged to hunt big cats, like this leopard, with cameras.

Trade in death

Most of us are quite unaware of the horrific traffic in wild animals. When you travel by 'plane or ship, you probably don't think of the animal cargo that might be carried. In fact thousands of animals, alive or dead, are transported across the world like this. Trade in animals is often unnecessary. The trade in luxury goods, like fur coats, is an obvious example.

Luxury furs

Of the 36 kinds of wild cat, over half are being exploited by fur traders. Cheetahs, snow leopards, tigers, ocelots and jaguars are just some of the big cats threatened like this. By the 1960s some of the larger cats had become so rare that traders turned to smaller ones like the South American margay or the Asian leopard cat. In Britain laws ban the import of *all* wild cat skins. Other countries are not so strict and there is a lot of smuggling.

Feathers for my lady

The demand for some feathers varied with fashions. Between 1890 and 1929 over *50,000 tonnes* of feathers were imported into France for high fashion clothes. *This* trade has stopped, but today Japanese people will pay high prices for the beautiful feathers of the bird of paradise.

The main trade today however, is in

Packed in crates with no room to move and not enough air to breathe, these two tigers suffocated in shipment. Animals sent by air can also die if kept in unpressurized or unheated cargo holds. Regulations exist to stop this, but small airlines often ignore them as penalties are small.

live birds for zoos or as exotic pets. India is one of the main exporters of live birds, though it has recently banned the export of the talking mynah which is much prized as a pet.

Tortoises

Another persecuted animal is the tortoise. It seems harmless to keep a pet tortoise, but in fact only 1 per cent of tortoises imported into Britain survive their first winter here. People often think that the tortoise 'sleeping' in the garden shed is hibernating. It is probably dead. Tortoises come from Greece, Turkey and North Africa where their numbers are steadily falling. They are packed tightly together for export and many die on the way. Dead ones are sold for their shells or to make souvenirs.

Tortoises can spread food poisoning and other exotic wild animals may also carry diseases. In itself, this is a very good reason for not keeping them as pets. Animals from other countries will probable find our country very unnatural as a habitat. By keeping these animals as pets you may be helping them become rare in their native countries. Once they are in our country they may soon die in the unnatural habitat.

Animals for belts and combs

Trade endangers many other animals. Snakes, lizards and crocodiles are slaughtered to make their skins into shoes and handbags. Sea turtles are hunted for their shells to make combs and spectacle frames. We have already seen the sad list of things whales are used for. Like so many other animals mentioned, their deaths are unnecessary.

All these goods, from fur to margarine, can involve the death of a rare animal. All could be manufactured from man-made, farm or vegetable products.

39

Breeding and reintroduction

It is a lot easier for man to wipe out animals than save the remaining rare animals. Let us see what is involved. It is not always hard to breed rare animals in zoos. Zoologists have learnt much about breeding wild animals. Rare Madagascan lemurs and Indian rhinos are just two animals that have been bred in zoos thousands of kilometres from their home lands.

Take the animals back home!

One way to save animals is to reintroduce them to their original wild habitats, but there can be problems. Perhaps the wild habitat no longer exists, or has become too dangerous for the animal's survival.

Scientists and educated people are concerned for animal welfare in distant countries. The problem is making local people in these countries share this concern. Local people are often very poor. *They* must struggle to survive. What we see as a rare bird may be just another meal to a local villager.

Breeding in the wild

These plans to help animals are expensive. North American experiments to conserve the whooping crane succeeded partly because the bird came from North America in the first place. Probably as important, though, was the fact that enough people were interested in and prepared to pay for the idea.

Breeding programmes in the harshest environments are more likely to work than those in foreign zoos. Orang-utans are successfully reared in the dense Indonesian jungles, though the destruction of these forests is a dangerous threat.

So there are two different approaches to breeding animals. Successful zoo breeding means animals are secure and do not die out forever. But zoos must be run responsibly. They must *not* be simply places for people to stare at strange animals. It would be best if we did not need zoos to save animals and could instead preserve the original wild animal habitats.

The North American whooping crane is one of the world's rarest birds. Only about 70 of these beautiful birds are left.

▲ Extinct in its native China, Pére David's deer owes its life to the 11th Duke of Bedford who, seventy years ago, collected these deer from European zoos and set up a breeding herd on his estate at Woburn.

Cousin Island, one of the Seychelles group in the Indian Ocean is a wildlife paradise. It was bought by the International Council for Bird Preservation in 1969. It now protects such rarities as the Seychelles brush warbler, the Seychelles fody, millions of seabirds and the last surviving specimens of the Seychelles giant tortoise. ▶

What you can do to help

By the time you have grown up, some of the animals mentioned in this book will be extinct. This is very sad and unnecessary, but it is not too late to help the plight of other animals.

What happened to the pond at the end of your road?
You can do a lot of good by working to help animals in your own area. We have mentioned animals in danger in far-away places, but find out what is happening in your own area. Perhaps a pond is being filled-in or used as a rubbish dump, perhaps woods are being cut down. Each year in England alone 33,000 hectares of land disappear under concrete. With them go wild flowers, insects, birds and small mammals. Many organizations are trying to preserve our wildlife, but not enough young people are involved. In most English counties there are Naturalists' Trusts interested in the wildlife of their particular area. They own and look after nature reserves. To do this they need help in running them and raising money to buy more wild areas. Your local library will help you get in touch with the nearest trust.

A nature reserve in your garden
If you live in a town, ask your teacher to take you to a local park. Even in cities there is a lot of wildlife, especially birds, to be seen. For example, a few miles from the centre of London, at Hampstead Heath, you can see the great crested grebe. This beautiful waterbird has a fascinating courtship display. Gardens or wasteland can be just as interesting. A magazine called *Oasis* tells you how to encourage animals into your garden. You can attract birds and bats by putting up special boxes for them. Butterflies and moths will visit flowers you grow in your garden. Gardens are very important for wildlife. In total area they are England's largest nature reserve.

Discover what is happening around you
What do you eat? What clothes do you wear? What animals were involved? Keep a special look out for

Pass the message on! Join a wildlife club or society and wear their badge—a simple way to help wildlife.

anything that uses whale products.

Above all, *find out more about animals.* Read about them, watch them in television wildlife films. Write to the people who make these films if you have any questions.

Try and get out more often into the country. If you like fishing, watch out for waterbirds and small mammals like voles. Even dragonflies are getting less common than they used to be. But, if you *do* fish, *never* leave your old nylon lines around. They can trap or strangle birds and mammals.

If you have a holiday by the sea take a look at the shore-life. If your beach is polluted, try and discover where the rubbish or oil came from. If you visit a farm, ask the farmer what fertilizers and chemicals he uses. Ask him which pests he is trying to kill and how much spray he uses.

Perhaps you could start a nature conservation club at school. Just thinking and talking about the world you live in is one of the many ways *you* can help.

DOS AND DONTS: OBSERVE WILDLIFE WITHOUT DESTROYING IT!
1. Don't leave litter. It is unsightly and small animals like mice or lizards can suffocate in old bottles or cans.
2. Don't pick flowers until you know if you may. Some plants are protected by law.
3. Don't disturb bird's nests or their eggs. Don't take young animals away from where you find them. They can look after themselves.
4. Do enjoy the country. Walk, climb or play in it, but leave it as you found it for others to enjoy it.

A 'Greenpeace' ship stops a Norwegian ship of seal hunters during the 1978 'Save the Seal' campaign.

Books to read

The Red Book of Animal Stories, Ed. by Andrew Lang; C.E. Tuttle 1972
Saving Our Wildlife, J.J. McCoy; Macmillan 1970
Wildlife of South America, Dorothy Shuttlesworth; Hastings 1974
Wildlife of North America, George F. Mason; Hastings 1966
Animal Rescue: Saving Our Endangered Wildlife, William Wise; G.P. Putnam 1978
Endangered Plants, Dorothy C. Hogner; Thomas Crowell 1977
Wild Flowers, John Gilmour and Max Walters; Collins-World 1976
City and Suburb: Exploring an Ecosystem, Laurence Pringle; Macmillan 1975
Understanding Ecology, Elizabeth T. Billington; Frederick Warne and Co. 1971
It's your Environment: Things to Think About, Things to Do, Environmental Action Coalition Staff; Charles Scribner's Sons 1976
Birds, Neil Ardley; Silver Burdett 1980
Deserts, Patricia Monahan; Silver Burdett 1980
Magazines:
Environment 4000 Albermarle St. NW, Washington, DC 20036
National Wildlife and International Wildlife National Wildlife Federation Membership Services 1412 16 Street NW, Washington, DC 20036
Audubon National Audubon Society 950 Third Avenue New York, NY 10022

Things to do and places to go

Get out into the countryside and look at the wildlife around you. One very good way to do this is to visit wildlife preserves or nature centers near your home. Many of these places offer guided tours and lectures. Your local library is a good place to find out about these places.

There are many excellent zoos you can visit. These include The Brookfield Zoo (near Chicago); The Milwaukee County Zoo (Wisconsin); The National Zoological Park (Washington, DC) The San Diego Zoo, and The San Diego Wild Animal Park (California). If you write these institutions you may find that they have special clubs for young people to join.

Many large cities have natural history museums. These museums will usually arrange guided tours and films and lectures for young people. Smaller local museums often have exhibits that show you what your area was like before it became built up.

There are many clubs and organizations whose main concern is conservation. These include the World Wildlife Fund (1319 18th St. NW, Washington, DC 20036); The Sierra Club (530 Bush St., San Francisco, CA 94108); The National Wildlife Federation (1412 16 St. NW, Washington, DC 20036).

Friends of the Earth (529 Commercial St., San Francisco, CA 94111) can help if you are concerned about international problems, such as whale hunting.

Some of the books listed here will give you lots of ideas for projects you can carry out at home, in the garden, or at school. Your local library will have many more interesting books on the subjects that have been mentioned in this book. Libraries will also be happy to help you get in touch with any local conservation groups, zoos, or nature reserves.

A danger list

92 endangered animals are mentioned in this book.

There are actually about 1,000 mammals, amphibians, reptiles and birds in the world in danger of extinction today.

In 1975 the World Wildlife Fund printed a list of animals and plants in danger. It included *839* kinds of animals and 68 different plants. The list was printed on both sides and was over 1½ metres long! This list only included the animals actually in danger of extinction. If it had included animals in slightly less danger, the list would have been many, many times longer. There is not enough room on this page to print the whole list. All we have been able to include are the large cats (tigers and so on) and the lemurs, monkeys and apes.

LARGE CATS

Eastern cougar
Clouded leopard
Formosan clouded leopard
Asiatic lion
Indian tiger
Caspian tiger
Siberian tiger
Javan tiger
Chinese tiger
Bali tiger
Sumatran tiger
Indochinese tiger
Leopard
Barbary leopard
South Arabian leopard
Anatolian leopard
Amur leopard
Sinai leopard
Snow leopard
Jaguar
Cheetah
Asiatic cheetah

LEMURS, MONKEYS AND APES

Black lemur
Red-fronted lemur
Sclater's lemur
Sanford's lemur
Mongoose lemur
Red-tailed sportive lemur
Nossi-bé sportive lemur
White-footed sportive lemur
Grey gentle lemur
Broad-nosed gentle lemur
Hairy-eared dwarf lemur
Fat-tailed dwarf lemur
Coquerel's mouse lemur
Fork-marked mouse lemur
Indri
Verreaux's sifaka
Perrier's sifaka
Western woolly avahi
Aye-aye
Golden lion tamarin
Golden-headed tamarin
Golden-rumped tamarin
Goeldi's marmoset

White-nosed saki
Bald uakari
Red uakari
Black-headed uakari
Woolly spider monkey
Tana River mangabey
Lion-tailed macque
Zanzibar red colobus
Tana red colobus
Uhehe red colobus
Olive colobus
Nilgiri langur
Golden langur
Pig-tailed langur
Snub-nosed langur
Douc langur
Kloss's gibbon
Pileated gibbon
Orang-utan
Chimpanzee
Pygmy chimpanzee
Gorilla
Mountain gorilla

Index

Illustrations appear in bold type.

Addax **20**
African wild ass 17, **17**
Age of Mammals 6
Antelope, giant sable **16**, 17
Avahi **27**

Biomes 9
Birdwing, Queen Alexandra's **12**
Bird of Paradise 38
Bison **6**, 14
Blackbuck **21**
Brazil 10

Canada 32
Capelin 29, 32
Cheetah 17, **17**, 36
Crane, Manchurian **24**, 25
  sandhill 24
  whooping 24, 25, 40, **40**
Crocodiles 39

Darwin, Charles 26
Deer, Pére David's 41
  pampas 15
Dinosaurs 6
Diseases 15, 39
Dolphins 30
  spinner 29
  spotted 29

Eagle, monkey-eating **13**
Ecology 8
Ecosystems 8, 9
Elephant bird **27**
Elephants 18, **18**, **19**
Energy cycle **8**
Environment 6, 7, 8

False sunbird **27**
Farming 6, 10, 14, 15, **15**, 18, 22, 23, 26, 34, 35, 36, 43
Feathers 24, 38
Ferret, black-footed 14
Fertilizers 23, 43
Finches 26
Fishing 28, 29, 32, 43
Forests 6, 10, **10**, **11**, 12, 27, 40
Frog, golden tree **13**

Fur coats 17, 36, 38, **39**

Gannet **29**
Gauchos **15**
Geese, white-fronted 23
Gibbon, pileated **13**
'Greenpeace' **43**

Habitats 8, 12, 40
Heron, squacco, 24
Hunting 6, 14, 16, 17, 18, **19**, 20, 21, **30**, 32, 33, **36**, **36**, 43

Ibis, glossy 24
India 21, 36, 39
Industrial Revolution **7**
Islands
  Cousin 41
  Galapagos 26
  Madagascar 27
  Mascarene 26
  New Zealand 26
Ivory 18, **19**

Jaguar 38

Keyna 16, 18

Leather goods, 39, **39**
Lechwe 23
Lemurs 27, 40
Leopard **16**, 17, 38

Mammoth **7**
Margarine 39
Margay 38
Marine Iguana **26**
Mynah, talking 39

National Parks 14, 16, 18, 24
Naturalists' Trusts 42
Numbat **21**

Ocelot 38
Orang-utan **12**, 40
Oryx, Arabian **20**
  scimitar-horned 20
Otter, giant **22**
  sea 33

Pelican
  Dalmation 24, **25**
  white 24, **24**

Pollution 23, 28, **28**, **29**, 43
Porpoises 29, 30
  Dall's **31**
Prairie Dog **14**
  black-tailed 14

Quagga **6**
Quetzal **12**

Rhea 15
Rhinoceros
  Indian 40
  Sumatran 12
  white 17, **17**

'Save the Seal' Campaign **43**
Seal, elephant 32, 33
  harp 29, 32, **32**
Sifaka **27**
Soil 8, 9, 10
Spoonbill 24, **24**

Takahe 26
Tigers 36, **36**, **37**, **38**
Timber 10
Toad, natterjack 34, **34**, 35
Tortoises 39
  Galapagos giant **26**
  Seychelles giant 41
Trans-Amazonica Highway 10, **11**
Turtles 39
  giant leathery 33
  green 33
  marine **33**

Uganda 18

Whales 30
  blue **31**
  fin 29, **31**
  humpback 30, **31**
  right 30
  sei **31**
  sperm 30, **31**
  white 30
Wolf, maned **14**, 15
Woolly spider monkey **13**
World Wildlife Fund 35, 36, 44, 45

Zebra 16
Zoos 20, 40, 44

46